JJ Waller's
Brighton
Vol:01

Introduction

It's a funny place, Brighton. A city on the edge of the country; a city that seems permanently on the razz; a magnet for hedonists, dreamers and other escapees from 'real life'. It's a destination you'll have heard about, even if you've never visited and you'll return to once you have. Because in Brighton's higgledy-piggledy blend of Regency stucco and fairground gaudiness, narrow lanes and rolling Downs, people lose their hearts. Here, they think, is the spot for me. Maybe they'll open a shop peddling pom-poms or a café selling cupcakes; write that book they've been talking about for years; learn to sail? It's a city that has invited people to project their dreams upon it since the dandy Prince Regent built his Indian-themed pleasure palace at its heart.

Everyone has a different experience here. "It's a hello-goodbye tinsel town," offered writer Des Marshall; "A love corner for slugs" pronounced Virginia Woolf. Keith Waterhouse perhaps came closest to summarising how many of us feel about the city: "Without putting a finger on it," he wrote, "you feel that Brighton is up to something."

We're the 'gay capital' of the UK, the most popular destination for hen nights, home of the World Naked Bike Ride and the World Beard and Moustache Championships. For a time we were deemed the UK's "most godless" city (and we were proud of that too). We sustain festivals and fringes, several theatres, weird shops, scores of pubs and an array of "characters", from showbiz faces to small-time crooks. We elected Britain's first Green MP. Yes, the city thinks it's terribly unique but let's be honest, it is.

How likely is it that a photographer can distill that elusive essence? In this book – the first of what is intended to be a series - photographer JJ Waller certainly comes close. He benefits from a lifetime keeping company with Brighton – one of the rare few that can genuinely call themselves locals – and like an old friend, his affection for the place is tempered with a clear-eyed objectivity. As a photographer, he acknowledges the obvious picture – the piers, the parties, the seaside gaiety - but hones in on a detail that shows Brighton beyond the picture postcard clichés; he captures the city with its make-up slightly smudged. He presents the city in its many guises, its quintessential Englishness and occasional otherworldliness.

His images are funny and unexpected - perhaps a legacy from his earlier years as a pioneering street performer in Brighton and London's Covent Garden. A discipline where the audience's attention must be earned and kept.

While his photographs appear spontaneous, they are the result of an insider's familiarity with a place and its moods. This approach of becoming 'invisible' to be 'present' is similarly reflected in his yet unpublished photo

JJ Waller's affection for Brighton is tempered with a clear-eyed objectivity. His pictures hone in on a detail that shows Brighton beyond the picture postcard clichés; he captures the city with its make-up slightly smudged.

documentary work made in nearby St Leonards on Sea. Here he has spent five years documenting the town's ongoing attempts at regeneration. His pictures evocatively show the daily journeys of the residents, the town's triumphs and small tragedies. Waiting patiently and recording what changes and what stays the same, he has become part of its fabric. "Making good pictures isn't about luck," he says, "It's about being there and following people's lives, visually exploring a place and developing a sensitivity to it."

But Brighton is a bit of a gift to a photographer. It's undeniably photogenic, its residents seem to step out of the house anticipating a photo shoot and, as Keith Waterhouse always suspected, it is usually up to something.

Whatever your experience of Brighton, this book invites you to think about it differently. Waller makes the familiar look strange and the ordinary extraordinary, with a twinkle in his eye and a smile on his face. After all, there's no point being here if you're not going to get into the spirit of things.

So slowly turn the page; spot the 'reveal'; linger on the faces; perhaps dream about what you would do if you lived here.

It's a funny place, Brighton, but to its residents and devotees, there's nowhere else quite like it.

Nione Meakin, September 2012

The beautiful thing about Brighton is that you can buy your lover a pair of knickers at Victoria Station and have them off again at the Grand Hotel in less than two hours.
Keith Waterhouse, Journalist and Author

Brighton's my home town. Whenever people come here, they have a good time. It's funny because you go to Blackpool – another seaside town - and everyone there wants to come to Brighton.
Tony Dunkley, Cleaner

Brighton is a city that gives the impression no one in it has a job. Beneath the surface, everyone is beavering away at something, but the overall illusion is of a place on a permanent holiday.
Lizzie Enfield, Author

You can't swing a paintbrush without hitting an art student, child busker or a skateboarding dog.
Grace Helmer, Illustrator

There are over 250,000 people in Brighton, Hove and Portslade, but you still bump into about ten people you know just going out to get a pint of milk. Julie Burchill, Writer

Wonderful community spirit, stunning landmarks, a unique sense of fun, the embracing of diversity all combine to make a fantastic city. I'm very proud to both live in and represent Brighton.
Caroline Lucas, Green MP

Brighton: not so much a city, more a geographical collection of outlandish haircuts.
Pete McCarthy, Writer

I've only been to Brighton once. Dreadful place, I'm a Hove man through and through, although I did live in St Leonards for a while. That's very nice. I'd recommend it. Do you have any photographs of Banksy's sandcastle in St Leonards? Roger Quimbly, Twitter Sensation

I fell in love with Brighton when she was a scruffy, naughty, disobedient place. Now we have grown up together and become more sensible, neater and more civilised but I still love her.
Adrian Bunting, Builder

In a city, you rarely bump into people you know. In a village, you always see the same people. Brighton's more like a town, a place where every day, you meet different people you know.
Peter Chrisp, Historian

OYSTERS

Great beer, great culture, and a football club we had to really fight to keep alive, which makes our recent successes even better. SEAGULLS! Attila The Stockbroker, Poet

I'll never forget Albion chairman Dick Knight getting a standing ovation at the Theatre Royal as he came into the royal box before the start of 'Brighton 'Til I Die!', pure magic.
Steve North, Actor and Albion Fan

You're looking through your car windscreen at hundreds of carefree people strolling along the sunny promenade. I'm looking through mine at the villain in their midst.
Detective Superintendent Roy Grace. Peter James, Crime Writer

Im 88
Im Gay
Im in love
I've no regrets

People come to this town and they say, "My God, I know why you live here"! People are so accepting and just love you for whoever you are. I've been here since the '60s - I'm nearly the oldest gay in the village. "Auntie" Roy, 75, The Brighton Tavern

I came to Brighton to get away from London, but it followed me.
Richard Paul Jones, Production Manager

A city made for bohemians - Where you can do just about anything and find a curious audience.
Neil Butler, Arts Event Producer

All the loose nuts roll down south.
Ian Smith, Artist

A German journalist once asked me why it said on all the books he read, "The author lives in Brighton". He was beginning to think it was code for something.
Lynne Truss, Journalist and Author

Brighton and me, well we're just the right fit. Both a bit tatty here and there, but with our heart in the right place. Sarah Hutchings, Artistic Director, The City Reads

I prefer Brighton at night because I love seeing all the different lights. I like driving down North Street and seeing the Wheel, or at Christmas, driving down under all the Christmas lights. I know it sounds sad but I just love it. Claire Dryden, Bus Driver/Conductor

Human nature doesn't change - like a stick of Brighton rock you bite it all the way down and it still reads 'BRIGHTON'!" Ida Arnold. Brighton Rock, Graham Greene, Writer

Since the '80s friends began moving to Brighton and I never heard from them again. So many people disappeared that I referred to the area as the Brighton Triangle. Now as a regular visitor I know why my friends didn't want to return to London. David Mc Gillivray, Screenwriter

Sunsets, outdoor living, seaside strolls, trendy boutiques, sunburned tourists, great pubs, nice cafes, yummy mummies, Guardianistas, seagulls, nights out ending at sunrise – make Brighton the best city in the country. Tim Ridgeway, Argus Journalist

Credits

Brighton for me is a seaside city, with cool people and The Lanes and two great piers (one of which is annually firebombed) and Sussex University and the skating rink where I did my first ever sliding on ice (Sugar Sugar was playing on the loud speaker) and sun and rain and a football team with a new stadium and all set right by the beautiful Downs – that I own (in my mind).

Eddie Izzard, Comedian

This book was never planned, at least not in the 'Lets do a Brighton book' kind of way. It came about because of the encouragement of friends who generously shared their enthusiasm for my images with their expertise and flair for taking risks. They gave me the motivation, guidance and unconditional support to make a Brighton book that would be a simple and fun chronicle of some of the people and events that go into making it the place that it is.

JJ Waller Nov 2012

Dedicated to the memory of Maurice Simmons & James Dimitri Georgiles

Published by Curious
www.curious-publishing.co.uk

Design: Transmission
www.thisistransmission.com
Print: Pure Print UK

All enquiries and print sales:
office@jjwaller.com

With Special thanks to
Jasmine Uddin
Nigel Swallow
Steve McNicholas
Bill Smith
Mohan Uddin
John Farquhar-Smith
Graham McDermott
Mick Perrin
Stuart Tolley
Nione Meakin
John Riches
Kate Strachan

Thank you to all the people that sent me quotes and kindly agreed to them being included in this book.

A catalogue record for this book is available from the British Library

ISBN 9-780957-439009